Tot and the Hawk

By Sally Cowan

It was dawn.

Big Jag did a big yawn.

"Wake up, Tot!" she said.
"Let's go hunting!"

Tot crawled up on a rock
by the creek.

She saw a fish jump.

She stuck out her paw to grab it.

But Tot was not quick!

Claud the big hawk
swooped down.

He got the fish in his
sharp claws!

Claud hauled the fish
up to a tree.

He ripped up the raw fish
with his claws.

"Bad luck, Tot!" yelled the hawk.

He did a cheeky squawk.

Tot was very mad.

"I'm so hungry!" bawled Tot.

"Don't bawl, Tot!" said Big Jag.
"The fish will swim away."

Tot stomped off.

She dug her claws into the bark of a tree.

Big Jag got a fish in her jaws.

"Try again, Tot!" she said.
"I will look out for that hawk."

Tot looked in the creek.

She saw a prawn crawl across
the creek bed.

Tot stomped her paw
on the prawn.

Claud the hawk swooped again!

But Big Jag did a big leap.

She **just** missed the hawk.

"The prawn is for Tot!"
hissed Big Jag to Claud.

The hawk flew off!

"Yum! Fresh prawn!"
said Tot.

She chomped it in her jaws.

CHECKING FOR MEANING

1. Who took Tot's fish? *(Literal)*

2. What did Tot end up eating? *(Literal)*

3. How would you describe Claud's character? *(Inferential)*

EXTENDING VOCABULARY

hauled	What did it mean when Claud *hauled* the fish up to a tree? When do we usually use the word *haul*?
squawk	What does *squawk* mean? What other animals squawk? What word could the author have used instead of *squawk*?
bawled	What is the base of *bawled*? How does adding –*ed* to the end of the word change the meaning? What other words have a similar meaning to *bawled*? E.g. cried, sobbed.

MOVING BEYOND THE TEXT

1. Where do you think Tot lives? Why?

2. What other foods might a hawk or a leopard eat?

3. What do you know about leopards? What else would you like to know?

4. What do you think might have happened the next time Tot was hungry?

DIPHTHONGS

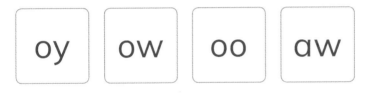

| oy | ow | oo | aw |

PRACTICE WORDS

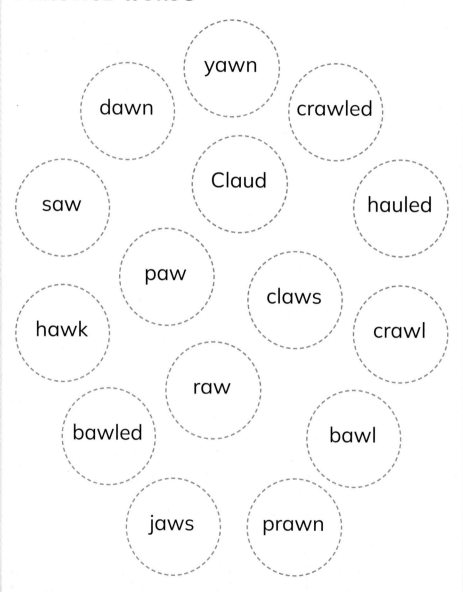

yawn

dawn

crawled

Claud

saw

hauled

paw

claws

hawk

crawl

raw

bawled

bawl

jaws

prawn